OVERCOMING SELF-ESTEEM PROBLEMS IN TEENS AND PRE-TEENS:

A PARENT'S GUIDE

BY DR. RICHARD L. TRAVIS

Thank you for purchasing this Book.

"Overcoming Self-Esteem Problems in Teens and Pre-Teens: A Parent's Guide"

Printed and bound in the United States

First Printing: 2014
Second Printing: 2016

ISBN-13: 978-1495214301
ISBN-10: 1495214303

www.rltpublishing.com

Special discounts are available on quantity purchases by corporations, associations, educators, and others. For details, contact the publisher at the above listed address.

Please Visit: **www.drrichardtravis.com/**

Introduction

Weekly, if not more frequently, we read of tragic shootings around the world. These tragedies and more are often linked to one person. The person responsible for these tragedies is quickly labeled mentally disturbed, or given some mental health diagnosis by the media. Often, as investigations continue, it is discussed that this person always had _low Self-Esteem_.

The term self-esteem is often confused or misunderstood. _Self-Esteem simply put is: "Your feelings, your appraisal, and your evaluation about yourself."_ You can have good self-esteem, and/or bad self-esteem. Some people actually have **no** self-esteem.

People with good self-esteem tend to be more self-confident. They tend to be happier and more easily attack the challenges of life. They are usually, but not always, less addictive. They are usually more motivated, and more assertive. They are also more receptive to others, and to discussing or hearing about new ideas.

People with unhealthy or "low" self-esteem" often have few friends, may isolate more, and have less success in school. Their social skills are often impaired, and success is also at a lower level than those who have healthy self-esteem.

This book is going to present to you the detailed differences between good (healthy) and bad (unhealthy) self-esteem. It also examines the development of self-esteem in children and the causes of good or bad self-esteem. As you read on you will find the characteristics of someone who has developed healthy or unhealthy self-esteem. You will find how someone's thoughts, positive or negative, can have a direct impact on their self-esteem development.

You will also find tips for parents to use in raising children with healthy self-esteem, and specific exercises to do with your children at home to start boosting self-esteem. At the end of the book you will find many Links, YouTube Videos, and Apps to give your much more ammunition in helping your child to develop a healthy sense of self and a positive self-esteem.

Table of Contents

What is The Definition of "Self-Esteem?"

Some call it self-concept, self-regard or self-respect, but whatever the name is; self-esteem is the summary of our thoughts and feelings that define our relationship with our abilities, our possibilities and ultimately ourselves as persons. Simply put, self-esteem is how we view ourselves.

We can gain self-esteem (good self-esteem) throughout our lifetime. (We also can gain an unhealthy sense of self, or low self esteem, as we age.) When we consider the ideal way good self-esteem develops, it should happen in childhood, but when we are more realistic, our self-esteem is a product of later life as well. Healthy or good self-esteem allows us to develop risk-taking ability, and the ability to build positive relationships.

Healthy self-esteem does not limit our actions because of fear. Healthy self-esteem allows us the hope and motivation to pursue dreams and desires, making good choices and trying to reach our goals. As we age, we can continue to improve our self-esteem through the positive experiences and social interactions of our life.

It is important to know that feeling good about yourself is no luxury, but an absolute necessity to have a healthy life. To improve our self-esteem we do not have to change others, which would be impossible anyway. We have to change ourselves--our way of thinking, and our attitudes.

What Creates High or Low Self-Esteem?

Pre-teens and teens can have various reasons to have problems with self-esteem. They might think that they are too fat, too dumb, too ugly or incompetent. They might also continually compare themselves to others. The development of self-esteem involves reactions from the environment. Parental influences, peer opinions and teacher judgments are the most important factors. The individual's own experiences are also crucial; successes and failures, the rewards and punishments we receive, and how others view us within a group. Sudden changes of behavior, mood swings, and unexplainable sadness are red flags suggesting low self-esteem.

Self-esteem has certain characteristics, which are the same for everyone. According to **Nathaniel Branden**, self-esteem has six pillars, which are practices for everyday life. These practices are actions we can take in day-to-day operations, which eventually become habits and a way of being.

The six pillars or practices of good self-esteem are:

- Conscious living.
- Accepting yourself.
- Being responsible to yourself.
- Being assertive.
- Living purposefully, and
- Having a personal integrity.

The actual level of self-esteem has its roots in many factors in youngsters. Low self-esteem can appear in certain situations only. For example, when teens or preteens are not comfortable or able to speak in front of a class it is an example of a lack of self-confidence or low self-esteem. It can also be a part of the person's character when it has effects that are more global, and it appears in a number of situations, as when your teenager thinks that no one loves her.

According to public opinion, a high level of self-esteem is one of the prerequisites to be successful and happy in our society, and consequently, low self-esteem in a certain way sets you up to be a failure and have dysfunctions later in life. Despite the relatively high self-esteem of America's youth, low self-esteem is the cause of many of our kid's problems today.

Some causes of low self-esteem are negative emotional responses, like criticism, teasing or punishment. In the case of children and teenagers, parents are not the only ones responsible in expressing these negative evaluations and feelings. Teachers, friends, and peers by their comments can also negatively affect the development of self-esteem of others.

If that is not enough, other factors from the broader environment of youth, like media, religion, sexuality, economic conditions, school failures and culture can also negatively influence how valuable the individual sees himself or herself. Considering all of these potential influences, it is easy to see that self-esteem is a very vulnerable construct. Given the many potential dangers, it might seem that a healthy and optimal level of self-esteem is very hard to build.

The concept of self-esteem is disputed by some for being a perception and not a reality. The same is true for the negative messages in childhood that influence the development of self-esteem negatively. The construct of; *the thoughts that we have today are due to the messages that we have received in the past does not have to be true. Despite that knowledge, these messages that we heard do have a powerful effect on us.*

Family or Parent's Role

The family is the first milieu to surround the child. It has effects on us practically from birth. We learn that the most important things in life are within our family, and that the basics of our self-esteem stem from the family. Our parents are the most important persons of our lives for several years, and they teach us many things; among them - the way we should see ourselves.

Spoken and unspoken parental evaluations of their children are greatly influencing the development of a child's self-esteem. Too many negative experiences and disappointments in the child's early years can lead to a disturbed sense of self. Parents' reactions and the quality of their care are the building blocks of the personality of children. These evaluations are especially important in early childhood, when the independent personality of children is forming. It is similarly very important in the sensible period of adolescence, when teens are trying to find out who they are and where their place is in the world.

Parents sometime use global words to describe a child as a complete being. He is "bad," because he is not able to play with other children at the playground, and destroys what others have built. He is "dumb," because he is unable to learn two lines for the kindergarten festivity.

The truth is, no child is born as "bad" or "dumb", but these negative evaluations lead to negative feelings within the child, and become parts of the forming identity of the child. Parents unconsciously or consciously plant negative seeds in their children. You can be sure that negative self-evaluations of six-year olds usually come from the spoken words of significant

6

adults. "I cannot sing," "I cannot draw," "I am bad," "I am clumsy." Be careful what you say, parents, as your child usually believes everything you say to be factual and truthful. If they believe what you say, then they will reinforce it with time to be absolutely true.

On the other hand, parents can build positive a self-concept in their child as well. Acknowledging your child's skills and abilities is extremely important. Positive reinforcement and feedback for adequate performances, and age-appropriate developmental tasks are great influences, which will shape self-image and self-evaluation in a positive way.

The parent's most important part in the development of self-esteem is probably their ability to serve as role models. The parent's attitude about themselves is often critical in the feedback given to their children. *For example, when a parent is constantly unhappy about his or her body or physical appearance, the child will most likely display the same attitude as a teenager.* It is important to learn to change things about us that we do not like and accept what cannot be changed.

Parental reactions to mistakes and failures of the child have a great influence. This is also mirroring the reaction to the parents own shortcomings. A little humor makes small errors easier to tolerate. Teenagers are especially likely to develop a negative voice within - "an inner critic." In many cases, this is based on the critical parent who they hear. Teens that feel that their parents have the qualities they admire, will develop a healthier self-esteem than those who do not feel like their parents have such assets.

The easiest way to build positive self-regard in our children is the use of compliments and rewards. It is hard to tell how much positive reinforcement is needed, as much of it depends on the personality of the child. It is vital that compliments are meaningful and not just empty phrases.

Positive reinforcement should focus on the concrete, and if possible, avoid a general compliment, e.g. do not say, "You are clever or nice." Instead of saying that, try to use phrases that are connected to the actual situation: "You put away the toys neatly," or "You did a great job with your homework."

Failures that your children experience are easier to accept, if you try to make your child a multifaceted personality. It would be great to help teach your child to be more tolerant of frustration. Praises should outweigh criticizing comments or critical observations. As a parent, it is important that you love your child with his or her mistakes and goof-ups, as well as when he/she is performing wonderfully.

The School's Role

School is an important place in the lives of children and adolescents, because they spend so much time there. Kids learn a great deal in schools, and during their years in formal education they learn much about themselves as well. For many of them, school is the first place where they face judgments and reactions from people who do not necessarily love, or have positive feelings toward them.

School is different from the family setting, because it is a place where the child or adolescent has to face expectations. These expectations often differ greatly from the expectations of the home, and to adapt to them is often difficult. To be able to achieve what is expected, children need a lot of learning, personal growth and development, and adaptation. School is a complex world, usually far more diverse than the home environment.

Having a good start in school is important to your child. If your child fits in, and is liked by teachers and peers, his or her self-esteem will be most likely good. If your child feels pressures are too hard to handle, or cannot progress and achieve what is expected, things might be worse. *If the initial adaptation is successful, the preteen or teen will find it easier to adapt to changes and multiple expectations from various teachers or new peers.*

Children in school have to adapt to other children as well. If your kid is able to form friendships and is generally liked by his peers, he will be able to tolerate negative reactions and judgments from some children. They need to learn that it is not possible that everybody will love you, and you do not have to love every single one in your environment.

Children have to learn to ignore the teasing from the **school bully**, because he often does not like anyone other than himself. A bully usually has complex problems with his personality, and it often stems from home. Teach your children that there is no relationship with what the bully says, and how you see yourself. He has a role: to hurt and tease. Teach your child that he does not have to play the bully's game and be the victim.

Help your child understand that they need good friends who value and appreciate them in their school. They should stay around the valued friends and students, and try to avoid negative students. Today's schools are much more sensitive to resolving issues of bullying quickly. So get the school administration involved if bullying does occur.

It is important that parents and schools regularly consult each other about certain matters. Apart from academic issues, questions of social development are crucial too. Parents need to know what happens with their child in school and how she feels there. A healthy self-esteem can be increased and reinforced through extracurricular activities which the child enjoys and can hopefully do well. Good schools offer a great variety of activities where children are able to show their talents. These opportunities can do wonders to develop positive self-esteem.

Society's Role

In our society of consumers, appearance and apparel are especially important. Young people, whose values are still developing, are particularly prone to believe in messages suggesting ideals which they will never reach. "You need to be this, or you need to be that; skinny, tall, or muscular." There is pressure for children to need to like certain things and reject others so that they can be "cool." They need to have things, new things, and expensive things! Consumer's views infect the minds of youth in many cases, and it leads to a decrease in self-esteem as well.

The truth is that it does not have to be this way. Society does a great deal to tear down the self-respect of teenagers. It fails to give enough positive models and conveys controversial expectations. Adolescents have limited access to select idols, which are positive personalities and exert a positive influence on their development. Society has no universally accepted values or guidelines to move development in a certain way.

Violence, sexual activities, and lack of respect for others are propagated in the media everyday. Society's message is to "make money and have fun." If you are unable to fulfill these requirements, you are not as worthy as you could be. It is very easy to buy into this misconception. Society often demands "market value" from us, its members. It is not important how good you are and what do you know, what matters most is how good are you in "selling yourself."

It is interesting however, that society expects us to make good choices, to be valuable and useful members and contribute to the greater good. Media examples that are more positive could make that much easier. It is very important that we filter the messages from society and the media. Many values are represented, and not every single one of them is useful for you and your child. For a child to find himself and to build his identity, he has to select from these societal values. Some help from a positive and responsible parent or adult to sift through these values can come handy in a child's decisions. It is very dangerous for them to build their self-esteem on values that are ultimately not theirs.

Church/Community's Role

In our society, we are members of several groups. We are students in our school, or workers in our workplaces, supporters of a team, or fans of a singer, or we belong to a church, scouts or chess study circle. The communities we belong to have significant effect on our self-esteem as well. Communities differ from schools or even families in the respect that in the majority of cases we decide to join them.

Our membership in groups is usually fairly straightforward; if we are happy in a community and feel that it contributes to our development, or simply enables us to feel acceptance and acknowledgement from others, we keep our membership in that group. If we feel that a certain group hinders our self-actualization, decreases our self-esteem, or makes us feel bad, we either leave that group or try to change it. Unfortunately a parent doesn't always know that their child is in a group that might hinder the growth of positive self-esteem.

Communities are an important part of our lives. They allow us a sense of belonging, look after us, and are intertwined with (optimally) positive interpersonal relationships. Positive and healthy communities have positive evaluations about themselves and about their members. These communities value the assets of their members and emphasize that they feel good as a member of the community. One of the most important communities in the lives of many is church.

Christian tradition puts great emphasis on spirituality, with modesty, as well as humility being key aspects of spiritual growth. Most Religious organizations warn against a focus on simply building self-esteem, and warn against complacency or arrogance.

A fulfilling life has three required essentials according to the teaching of most religions; **personal identity**, which is not to be confused with self-esteem. Personal identity refers to a proper assessment of our worth, not underestimating our value, but also not exaggerating ourselves. The other important factors are **deep faith** and **a sense of purpose and mission**. The religious teachings of having a realistic self-worth instead of pursuing a high level of self-esteem are in accordance with psychological findings. Religion does not require self-love, but demands love for God and for one another. **Pride** is not considered a good quality of someone who is following most religions.

Peer's Role

Peers have an important role in late childhood and adolescence. They are more and more indispensable in the lives of youth, and optimally they are helping our children to grow up. Friendships and romantic relationships with peers influence socialization, and affect interests and provide emotional support when needed. Friends are often the only ones who will listen to an adolescent, when often nobody else has time or interest.

Relationships with peers have a great influence on our self-esteem development as well. Not every peer is our friend, and not everybody loves us. School or playground bullies, malicious comments, or disregard to our abilities can negatively affect the way we view ourselves.

What your child needs to learn is that all those bad boys in school have serious trouble at home, and this is the reason behind their peculiar behavior. Children need to be encouraged to be bold and move away from friends that are filled with negative attitudes and negative behavior, and associate with people that have positive energy. Classmates with positive thinking will always show you the positive points, and support you in all your ventures.

Many children nurture a bad self-image because of poor choices in choosing friends. Your child's friends are a great influence on them, but ultimately they are the only ones that can make good decisions. Bad friendships will affect your child's ability to accept themselves for who they are, and interfere with being around people that appreciate your child for who they really are.

Remember, if someone constantly puts your child down and damages their self-esteem, he is not their friend.

The Characteristics of People with Healthy Self-Esteem

Nurturing a positive self-image has nothing to do with your looks, belongings or your parents' social status. The key in good self-image is accepting you as who you are. Feedback and judgments from others are an important influence, however you do have to deal with this feedback with some caution. It is more important to maintain a healthy level of self-esteem, even while considering everybody's opinions.

Self-esteem influences your relationships and your trust with other individuals. Positive self-esteem is associated with strength and flexibility; it allows taking control of your life and growing from your mistakes without fearing rejection.

Positive self-esteem has the following features:

- Confidence.
- Non-blaming behavior.
- Self-direction.

- Awareness of personal strengths.
- Ability to learn from mistakes.
- Accepting mistakes from others.
- Optimism.
- Problem-solving skills.
- Independence and cooperation.
- The ability to feel comfortable with a wide range of emotions.
- Trust.
- A sense of personal limitations.
- Good self-care.
- The ability to say no.
- The ability to like to meet new people.
- Not worrying about judgment from others.
- Having the courage to express themselves.
- Are willing to try new things.
- Make good leaders.
- Less mental health problems.

Someone with low self-esteem can be taught how to improve their self-image and raise their self-esteem. Low self-esteem does not have to be a lifelong curse. Unfortunately most people do little to change this aspect of their belief system, unless some tragedy forces them into therapy, or some chance viewing of a television show resonates with them to do something.

It is difficult to change old beliefs that we have about ourselves, but not impossible. Please do some research on Low Self-Esteem, Low Self-Image, or Low Self-Worth on the internet or at the local bookstore. You will find many sources of information and even directions you can take to improve upon your self-image.

The development of self-esteem does not make you over-confident, complacent or vain. It just allows you to accept and appreciate your talents, abilities or personal attributes. Self-concept has several links to self-esteem. If you constantly see yourself as a failure or a loser, it just feeds negative self-esteem and creates a negative attitude.

Healthy self-esteem requires a certain confidence about you. Self-confidence is the belief that you can succeed and are capable. Self-confidence is a perception of the self, just like self-esteem, but it relates to abilities. Self-esteem is, however, related to the individual's perceived worth or value. You need a certain level of confidence to be a positive person and to develop further. It is important to know that people with healthy self-esteem are not always overly confident, and they may not see their abilities realistically.

We need to reevaluate ourselves regularly and critically. Self-assessment needs to be accurate to offer us any help. Try to describe your weaknesses by using a non-pejorative (non critical) and accurate language, which is specific, and try to find corresponding strengths. The essence of self-esteem is having compassion for yourself, by forgiving mistakes, not having unreasonable expectations.

Self-esteem connects to values. When you have positive values, they allow positive self-valuation. The characteristics of good values are that they are flexible, realistic, life enhancing and based on one's own decision.

High self-esteem can work as a resource built from positive feelings that can be useful under certain conditions. It is also associated with more initiative. These two characteristics seem to be the best advantages of high self-esteem. It is helpful to focus on understanding ourselves accurately and honestly instead of only trying to build a high level of self-esteem.

Self-esteem in this sense could provide valuable functions and helpful (yet not always pleasant) information about the individual, instead of an inflated sense of self. An accurate self-evaluation could save a lot of time and effort, as well as disappointment. (Baumeister, et al, 2003)

https://www.youtube.com/watch?v=zq-fSpFhNYw **"3 Ways to boost your Self Esteem"**

https://www.youtube.com/watch?v=Oc-B536E6MY **"10 Tips for Improving Self Esteem"**

https://www.youtube.com/watch?v=FeLpvgAVtU8 **"Self Esteem Understanding & Fixing Low Self-Esteem"**

https://www.youtube.com/watch?v=AyIKj6R3axE **"How to Stop Caring What People Think"**

https://www.youtube.com/watch?v=dhuabY4DmEo **"How to Build Self-Esteem – The Six Pillars of Self-Esteem by Nathaniel Brandon. (Animated Book Review)"**

Can Good Self-Esteem ever be a Bad Thing?

People with high self-esteem usually think that they are more popular and have better social skills when compared to others with lower self-esteem. Evidence fails to support this claim. When rated by peers, individuals with high-self esteem are no more popular than others are with low self-esteem. They even might elicit negative responses from others, and alienate people with their inflated self-view.

Adolescents with high self-esteem can strengthen prosocial and antisocial tendencies as well, supporting initiative and confident action. Individuals with high self-esteem are likely to have more experience with sex and with drugs. They might also bully others or retaliate aggressively, if they feel attacked. (Baumeister et al, 2003)

Adolescents who have high levels of self-esteem might be well aware of their qualities, but they can be mistaken and act a little arrogant. Because self-esteem does not have to be realistic, high self-esteem does not guarantee you that others share your opinion about yourself. People who have a high level of self-esteem might often make the mistake of thinking they make a good impression, but the sad truth for them is that often they are neither nicer, nor more popular.

High self-esteem is certainly better than very low self-esteem, but too high a level of self-evaluation is no better than a relatively low level of it. Parents, teachers and other relevant figures from the social environment have a responsibility to **not** plant the seeds of self-loathing or self-hatred in the developing youth.

It is also very important that they do not convey messages that allow the forming of an individual whose self-evaluation is very high, but his or her self-concept lacks real foundations. Eventually these young people will face the truth, and might find it very hard to deal with it. Having a high-self regard does not necessarily mean that you have to be arrogant or narcissistic, yet despite that, you might fall.

Nick Hornby in his famous book **Fever Pitch** gives us a perfect example of this over-rated self-esteem. Self-belief and dedication to a cause can be viciously misleading, as Hornby points out. *"Arsenal had a player named Gus Caesar. He was far better than any other young boy in his school and miles ahead of the other boys in the district's selection. A very big team picked him up. He played for the reserves and suddenly he found himself in the first team. Playing for one of the biggest teams in England also opened the door for him to the U-21s, so he had every right to think that he is one of the best young English footballers and has a bright future in the game. He was dedicated, hard working and never complacent or arrogant. Sad for him, all the faith put in him by teachers, coaches or scouts was mistaken. He was simply unable to cope with the requirements of First Division football, and his shortcomings forced him to move to lower league clubs and finished his career in the football obscurity in Hong Kong. Caesar did nothing wrong by having a high self-esteem at the beginning of his Arsenal career. He had every right to do so. Reality had other plans however".*

23

The story is a perfect illustration of why should we be careful as parents or teachers in the building up of self-esteem in a child or teenager. We have no right to put someone down and destroy his or her fragile self-esteem, but false evaluations from the outside lead to a false evaluation in the individual and eventually disappointments will follow.

The Characteristics of Teens and Pre-Teens with Low or Unhealthy Self-Esteem

If you have low self-esteem, you are probably:

- Not believing in you.
- See yourself failing before you begin something.
- Find it hard to forgive mistakes.
- Believe you will never be as good as you should be.
- Are afraid of showing your creativity.
- Feel dissatisfaction with life.
- Are spending most of the time alone.
- Are complaining and criticizing too much.
- Are worrying about everything and doing nothing.
- Have more mental health issues.
- Treat yourself badly, but not others.
- Are expecting less from life.
- Are not fair to yourself.
- Are reluctant to take challenges.
- Disregard your positive qualities.
- Use negative words to describe yourself.
- Blame yourself when something goes wrong.

- Are concerned what others think about you.

Low self-esteem can make life extremely painful. It can lead to feelings of being a victim, or feeling out of control. Poor or low self-esteem also causes internalization of the criticism from others. Low self-esteem decreases happiness and reduces initiative.

Can Low Self-Esteem ever be a Good Thing?

In truth, nobody likes someone who has *extremely* low levels of self-esteem, but having a somewhat lower level of self-esteem does not mean that nobody will ever like you. Low self-esteem is usually associated with negative things, but this is not necessarily true. *A realistic, but low self-esteem might mean that you are aware of your shortcomings and actively work on them to be better.* Low self-esteem can also represent modesty and humility. These are characteristics, which cannot be considered to be negative.

Low self-esteem is more common in some cultures that value the "collective" above the individual. The question is not what you think about yourself and how high your self-evaluation is, but rather than how useful you are to your community and society. To put it simply, low self-esteem can be just due the fact that you are not obsessed with yourself, but focus on other things.

Although low self-esteem is commonly associated with doing bad things, it is not always true. Children or teens whose self-esteem is lower are unlikely to be bullies or abusers. However, they are often the victims of bullies. Those who have high level of self-esteem and think they are "a gift to humanity," might get easily offended, if they are not treated like royalty. On the contrary, people with a lower level of self-esteem are unlikely to have such thoughts.

Self-Esteem's Effect on Mental Health and Medical Conditions

Self-esteem is constantly associated with mental health problems, or with the lack of them. It can also present a problem to our mental health. Both overly high and pathologically low levels of self-esteem are unhealthy. Low self-esteem is a cause for anxiety and depression by many. These problems feed off each other in a vicious cycle; the lower your self-esteem, the more depressed and anxious you are - and then this lowers your self-esteem even more.

As for medical conditions, self-esteem can have a direct effect on physical health, but indirect symptoms can also happen. Individuals with low levels of self-esteem are more likely to be unhappy, anxious or depressed. These symptoms actually can cause physical effects on the individual's health. Low self-esteem makes people prone to have psychiatric conditions, particularly depressive eating or substance abuse disorders. These physical or mental health disorders can lower the level of self-esteem even further.

To avoid illnesses or protect yourself against health endangering factors, a positive outlook and a good degree of optimism are very potent attitudes. Better levels of self-esteem are associated with more happiness and optimism. Therefore we can assume that a positive outlook of oneself is coupled with a positive outlook on life, and this is related to better physical and mental health.

Children or Teens

The feeling of incompetence can become a belief deeply rooted in your heart. If you have the assumption that you are incompetent and encounter situations which nurture this assumption, you will probably expect the worst results, and your performance might really suffer.

One example of this might be the extreme fear of solving a task in front of your class. Avoiding the triggers that elicit the feelings of incompetence does not help either, because once you withdraw from a difficult situation, you just reinforce your thought that you are unable to deal with it. What you have to do in such situations is to find the unique features of the situation, and not rely just on your previous experiences of failure.

Teenagers and adults are likely to have a poor body image if they have low self-esteem. Low self-esteem causes more sensitivity, which means you tolerate criticism less, or are easily offended. It makes you more prone to feel fear and anxiety.

Adults

Erol and Orth (2011) are of the opinion that low self-esteem is a risk for negative outcomes in adolescence and young adulthood. Emotionally stable, extroverted and conscientious individuals have higher levels of self-esteem compared to their peers with emotional instability, introversion and less confidence. In addition, high levels of mastery, low risk-taking and better health predict better levels of self-esteem.

Baumeister (2005) notes that low-self esteem was thought to have been the cause of violence, criminality or aggression. This assumption is not true however. Aggressors have in many cases very high opinions of themselves. Self-loving brutes, violent gang members, playground or school bullies, or even tyrants like Hitler or Stalin have had little or no negative self-esteem.

The constant negative feelings, which come with low-self esteem, make your life harder than it should be. A low level of self-esteem negatively influences our relationships. You are most likely afraid to try new things, because you doubt your abilities to be successful. This attitude will make you fail and if you do so, your original thought is justified--"you were right, you should not have tried it in the first place." You forget the fact that others who are actually successful also fail sometimes, but they see failures as steps on the road to success. Parents can really have a great deal of influence on their children when trying to show examples of famous people, or people in the news who have failed at great things, and yet turned things around and became great people.

Another issue with low self-esteem and mental health is the issue of **perfectionism.** "Everything you do must be perfect; otherwise, it is not good enough." *This personality trait will cause you a lot more trouble than you might think, especially in your social life. Remember the words of Salvador Dali, who said that "you do not have to be afraid of perfection, because you will never achieve it."* You do not have to be afraid of perfection either. Good enough is enough!

Self-esteem that is too high just might cause you severe problems---just think about the worst performers of the various televised talent contests. They are self-assured and dare to perform in front of a national public, but they are ridiculed in front of millions.

The world is full of misunderstood geniuses, whose self-esteem might be sky-high, but no one appreciates them. They are convinced however that everyone else is to blame. Where does this false sense of accomplishment or talent or brilliance come from?

Why is your Child not Confident?

Parents ask this question frequently of themselves. Self-esteem is about having a positive view about yourself and the situations that you may come across. Typically, with good self-esteem, you do not fear any challenges, are able to stand by your belief, have enough courage to accept responsibilities, and identify your limitations.

Children might work slightly differently however. They might be offended or negatively influenced by things adults do not care about.

Here are some reasons why your child may not be confident enough to face other people.

Addressing - Sometimes the way you address your child may seem funny to you, but your child may not take it the way you think. Phrase or statements like "Hey you dumbo," and "Are you stupid?" "What kind of an idiot are you?" "Don't act smart in front of me," are lines which parents might use with their adult friends, and sometimes use the same lines with their children, not intending any harm. Over time this is enough negative labeling for a child to become extremely distressed, depressed and discouraged.

Remember, kids do not know the world enough yet, and might not be able to distinguish between a joke, a silly line, or serious talk. There is great power in the words because they come from mom and dad. Preteens and teens might be sensible and do not take harsh words kindly. So next time you feel that you are about to fill up your conversations with simple "fillers" like these, you need to realize that you might just destroy your child's self-confidence. Address your child with respect, as you would expect that to be done to you.

Comparison – Parents always want their children to stay ahead of the other children in the neighborhood and at school. Every time your child brings home low grades, the first thing you tend to ask or tell is "*What grade did Harry get?*" "*Learn something from Harry!*" "*Harry is better than you.*" While all of these sentences might make parents believe that their children may get competitive and bring better grades than Harry, what actually happens is that you are hurting your child's self-esteem. This makes him feel that he is not as good as Harry, and to you, "Harry is the best in the world!"

The fact is that Harry is not your child, and you should not be concerned about his performance. You should judge your child or teenager based on his or her abilities and efforts. If you have to compare, compare the current performance or behavior to a previous one. Notice developments, acknowledge greater knowledge or better skills, but warn against underachieving based on the kid's own standards.

Likewise, parents always tend to compare their children to their siblings, which again leads to low self-confidence, and to various negative emotions like jealousy, anger and revenge. Parents unknowingly may commit such mistakes without realizing that they are actually drilling a deep hole for a darker side in their children. Comparison with siblings may be extremely fruitless and painful.

Every parent knows that no two children are the same, not even monozygotic twins. Siblings have different developmental rates, distinct strengths, weaknesses, and different personalities. Siblings are important persons in each other's lives, but as a parent, you need to know that they are also rivals with each other in a certain sense – namely for the love, affection and attention of parents. *It is a cliché, but it is true, you cannot compare apples and oranges.* The sibling, who is negatively affected by the comparison, will have a tough time to live up the expectations of the parents, while the compliment can make the other child complacent.

School pressure - We all know how important school is for children. Although he spends only certain hours of the day in school, it is one of the most significant places for the child to learn. However, with school comes along a great deal of peer pressure, teacher's pressure, study tension, social embarrassment and teasing. Not all children go through the same situations, but several studies have shown that at least one out of three kids face serious negative influences from school.

The reasons for these negative influences could vary. For example, your child's friend prefers somebody else as his favorite. Perhaps your child's teacher may have a habit of scolding your child and embarrassing him in front of his classmates. Sometimes your child may not be able to cope with the study pressure present at school, and may become an introvert. With these kinds of influences he cannot achieve good grades or answer questions properly in class, and may even nurture a negative reinforcement of his behavior.

It is vital that parents keep a close watch on the school activities of kids, and know about their child's progress in every phase of his life. The best way to know this is to engage yourself in conversations with your children, and ask them how they feel about going to school. Get to know if they have any pressure or tension that they cannot deal with at school. As the experienced person who always keeps the best interest of your child first, you should be able to help him/her somehow.

Some children do not show any interest in studies and other activities. This point is probably also well known to parents of children whose self-esteem suffers. Just like adults who go through depression and stress, children are also bound to have such emotions when they have low self-confidence. The psychological functioning of children and teenagers is highly complex, and they need the help of their parents to come back from low self-confidence. Children with low self-esteem foster many unhealthy behaviors which may be defense mechanisms that they build to save themselves from social embarrassment.

For instance, if your child has knowingly committed a mistake and he knows that you are about to scold him, take note of his behavior. You might notice that before you even start a conversation, your child starts to blame others for his mistake, or sometimes tries to hide from you to avoid a conversation.

On the other hand, parents who force their children to bring home good grades, may be in big trouble if children cannot cope with the standards set by parents. (Don't be surprised if in the next report period you might find an altered grade report from your child.) In the attempt to make their children competent, parents may actually make children sly, cunning, and manipulative, which may again develop into serious social issues when they grow up.

Bad company - Another reason why your child may have low self-esteem may be that he/she is in the company of children who are a bad influence. Friends are the most important priority in your child's life at a certain point, and if these friends do not present good values, chances are that your child may suffer from various negative or conflicted emotions, along with low self-confidence. It is crucial that you must always keep a watch on what kind of company your child keeps, and where they go all the time. As a parent, you are wise to get familiar with your kids' friends and their backgrounds. Take the time to get to know your child's friends and possibly their families.

A child takes a while to develop destructive behaviors, but some simple initial symptoms that you could notice are the following:

- Not showing enough interest in studies,
- Not interested in playing with friends,
- Making an attempt to hide from people,
- Not making direct eye contact,
- Always trying to defend himself,
- Blaming others for even the slightest mistake,
- Making excuses for lack of responsibility,
- Lying,
- Stealing,
- Cheating,
- Developing destructive behavior,
- Purposely trying to stay lonely.

These are the initial symptoms that you may notice as a change in your children's behavior. This could indicate that they could be in the phase of transforming themselves from an energetic young child to a destructive loner. This is exactly the time parents should step in and act to help solve their problems.

You might have a short time to intervene, but you do have the opportunity to help your child become a "normal," happy kid, or watch him lose confidence and possibly even become self-destructive.

How does Negative Thinking Influence Self-Esteem?

Our thoughts have great power. They are able to shape us in one way or another. Our thoughts influence the way we view the world. If we think negatively, we give off a negative "vibe," and we might view the world as a negative place. These negative feelings and thoughts are especially likely to be repeated when you are not feeling well or having a bad day.

It is important that you pay attention to these thoughts of your children and be aware of them. While these thoughts exist and they bring the child down, even unconsciously. Negative thinking can be a self-fulfilling prophecy. The thinking does not have to be based on fact for it to become true to the child. It is useful however, if you do some analysis and decide whether there is any truth in the negative thought patterns.

Technique: *If you have the feeling of being stupid or a jerk and nobody will ever like you, think about it: would you say that to another person? If not, why do you keep saying it to yourself?*

To avoid negative thoughts, you must replace them with more positive thoughts and ways of thinking. Thoughts create feelings, and feelings create emotions. Emotions then create behaviors. Do you see where negative thinking might go? It might not be easy, but there are definitely some ways to change this negativity.

The influence of others could offer valuable help. Ask someone who likes you, and whose judgment you trust, what they think or feel about whatever the negative thought is that you are having.

Their perspective could really help interrupt the continuation of this negative thinking.

Negative thoughts are connected to negative words. Stop using them! Replace negative words with positive expressions. **"No, never, don't, worried, would, and should," can be replaced by "I, me, my, happy, could, and would be nice."** The positive thought(s) should be repeated over and over to take the place of negative feelings.

It is interesting, but even body language or a facial expression has an effect on our mood and feelings. In a research study, people were asked to hold a pencil between their lips (which is similar to the facial expression of sadness) or between their teeth (which actually makes them smile). Those people in the study who had a forced smile actually felt much better and experienced far more positive thoughts and judgments. Try this experiment yourself and then with your children.

Smiling reduces stress and anxiety, makes you look more attractive to others. It changes your mood for the better, and releases hormones in your body that are associated with good feelings.

Negative feelings about ourselves and negative thinking consume a great deal of our energy. Remember, this energy can be put to better use instead of making you feel even worse than you actually do.

What Differences Exist between Self-Esteem Development in Boys and Girls?

Boys and girls have different socialization during their development, face different expectations, and fulfill different roles. It is a widespread belief that young adult or adolescent males have higher levels of self-esteem. Scientific research has found no such disparities between genders. Boys and girls have usually no differences in their self-esteem.

When considering the effect of gender, the main difference between the self-esteem of females and males is the fact that girls are less satisfied with their body. They are more often thinking that they are fat or otherwise less attractive, but they do not think they are less able socially, less intelligent, or have less chance to succeed. (Baumeister, 2005)

Another significant difference between boys and girls is that females are more likely to be affected by media influences.

Any differences between the self-esteem of an average girl and boy are not significant statistically. There can be great individual variations of course. A word of caution is appropriate if we warn against the well-intended, but there is a false belief that adolescent girls have a serious problem with their self-esteem.

The fact is that they have no more trouble with their self-esteem than adolescent boys do.

The only significant difference is the area of self-confidence. Certain topics are more sensitive for girls, while others are more concerning to boys, but he overall level of their self-esteem is not showing the differences that many believe. Girls and boys are equally confident. If we want to address the issue of low self-esteem, we do not have to deal with that question gender-specifically. Children and teens, who suffer from low self-esteem, are struggling with similar problems.

Tips and Techniques for Parents

Self-esteem is greatly influenced by the significant people in children's lives. Parents, teachers or peers can make a dramatic impact on a child's value of his or her self, and can determine for a long time how that child values himself or herself. This book has already presented what not to do as a parent or a teacher, now let us just talk about opportunities that are more positive. See how you can help turn the development of the self-esteem of a child or teenager into a more positive direction.

What you do as a parent to help your child depends on many things. The age of your child, his or her personality, your personality, your way of parenting, cultural influences, economic conditions, and many more factors affect the possibilities to enhance the level of self-esteem in your child. Therefore, it is almost impossible to give personalized advice for everyone within the limits of this book. Some of the tips are already presented in other sections of the book, but we have collected them here for your convenience.

- Be a positive role model. The way you handle yourself and your affairs is the most important model for your child. Make it a positive one.

- Be careful with your words. Kids are sensitive and might take your careless phrases to heart. Do not say things that you do not mean.

- Show love and affection for your child. You do not have to make their ego too inflated, but praise and compliment your child as much as possible.

43

- Provide feedback which is accurate and positive. This is particularly useful when you praise effort. Results are important, but to learn hard work and dedication is probably even more important. Teach your child to make every effort and try as hard as possible.

- Help identify negative thinking patterns and beliefs. Children are not necessarily always correct in their evaluation of themselves and their environment. You can help them a great deal by identifying irrational beliefs and replacing them with realistic views.

- Create an environment at home which is safe and loving. It speaks for itself and should not be a question. Provide clear rules and boundaries, have realistic expectations, encourage age-relevant developmental tasks, offer your time, and provide support and supervision.

- Allow your child to participate in activities that boost self-esteem. Extracurricular activities, assignments at home, various forms of self-expression, like opportunities for athletic or artistic talent, and hobbies give children the chance to find and cultivate talent, which is good for your child.

- Emphasize communication. In many cases, adolescents and their parents feel that they have lost each other and a world separates them. Do not let this happen. Communicate regularly and appropriate to the development of your child.

- Show respect for your child and for his or her identity. Your child is not you. He or she might like different things or have different priorities. Also, consider age as a factor. Do not treat your 16 year old as a 10 year old, because she will not like it.

- Help your children build up the skill of effective time management. Children and particularly adolescents often struggle with the adequate use of their time. (Parenthetical comment: it might be even useful for you also, if you also struggle with it.) You may want to read more about this topic of time management.

- You can be critical, but be reasonable and just. Be prepared to accept opinions from children, especially from adolescents who have a very concrete opinion about the world. They have to learn to express themselves accordingly, and without hurting others. A great model for them is the way you distribute your criticism. Take their opinions and feelings seriously.

- Make sure that your child can count on you. Kids are likely to do things they would like to forget about10 years later, and will probably not be proud of them. Your child is your responsibility, even if he did something "stupid." You do not have to be happy about it, but it is important that you support him, and be behind him.

- Avoid comparison with siblings and peers. Each child is different and has his own strengths.

- Positive reinforcement and praise can be public, but disagreements and corrections have to be dealt with in private. This is very important….

- Most importantly: **Be There!!!!**

Training Can Improve The Self-Esteem of Your Child

Training your child means making him realize the difference between right and wrong. This indirectly makes your child a good citizen and an accepted person in society. This can also lead to a self-confidence boost in your child, and help him to move forward in life.

Uncertainty pulls a child away from society. He or she is not sure whether he/she is right or wrong, so in the attempt of avoiding any social embarrassment, they may become introverted with low self-esteem. However, children who have been trained to face the world and confront situations with the right solutions will have more self-esteem.   This is because they know what to do and when to do the right thing. This confidence is what children need to progress in life and make the best out of each situation. This self-confidence also helps them avoid problems, and find the right solution(s) to handle negative situations.

Choosing to train your child is one of the best gifts that you could give him/her, as your children are the reflection of you and your perception of life. A self-confident child can do a great deal when it comes to achieving success in life and making a great career of his/her own. It is extremely important for parents to train their children before they enter into the real world and face new challenges.

How Do You Train Your Child For Real World Challenges and Improve Self-Esteem?

Teaching responsibility is often considered one of the most important tasks put upon a parent. As a child learns to be responsible, there is evidence that self-esteem improves. Irresponsibility in teenagers is known to be one of the most common problems of modern adolescence. Even if a young man or young lady is chronologically ready to face the world if their parents would not be around to launder, cook or even lend them money to go shopping, are these youngsters ready to face the real world?

Gone are the days when schools were responsible for teaching homemaking skills, life organization and money management. Today parents bare the sole responsibility of training their child to face real world challenges, and to understand that with life, along comes certain responsibilities.

This does not mean that children should be deprived of playing games, but it's the balance between fun and responsibility that meets the guidelines laid down by parents.

Homemaking skills - You cannot send your child out into the world where all he learned to do was scatter his clothes around, leave unattended dishes and keep the house messy. All of this shows the way he or she had been trained at home. This is exactly the reason chores make the perfect training ground for homemaking skills, as even the youngest child can sort clothes, fold washed clothes and even put them into the closet.

By allocating such household chores, you are improving coordination skills. By the time your child approaches teenage years he/she can be much more independent. Other homemaking skills would be: spending time with parents when they do repair and maintenance, listening to phone calls made for cable service or electrical service problems, accompanying parents shopping at the drugstore, or hardware store. You could ask your children go with you to the hardware store, or ask them to observe how you perform certain other home tasks that he or she could learn to do own their own.

This basic involvement in cleaning up, cooking, preparing the laundry and maintenance gives way to some good conversations, socialization, kitchen safety and that of lessons on food and nutrition. You can see how all of these activities have the potential of developing a child's self-esteem to be very healthy.

Social skills - Yet another important skill that every young lady or gentleman is expected to have is exhibiting social skills that can make them acceptable in society. The best way to instill these skills is by educating your children in the relaxed atmosphere of your own home, so if they commit any mistake you are free to correct them. Parent's role modeling of good social skills is the greatest teacher to a child. A parent could also play certain games like having a tea party, or a special lunch, where your children are taught and asked to use their best manners. Table manners are important when a teen or child are at their first stay over at a friend's house.

While they serve you tea and exchange pleasantries, teach them about respecting others and what should they do when they are talking with adult family members. You may also actively introduce how to use some simple manners like: opening doors for others, saying "thank you," the use of the word "please," and simple listening skills.

Along with learning such responsibilities, they could also learn the consequences of their mistakes, which would be a reminder to them for any mis-steps. Reward based training will make them both accountable as well as personable. Again, the link to improved self-esteem is quite evident in these learning activities.

Perception of Life - It is important to teach children on how to progress in life in simple ways, be that in the form of answering phone calls, or navigating through the phone maze of talking to someone about your cable TV. Parents must teach their children how to steer clear of many dangers in life, and draw firm boundaries. They should know the difference between right and wrong, and keep information such as phone numbers, addresses and personal information, provided that they do not share it with a stranger.

Time Management – Children are the weakest when it comes to time management and learning the basic concepts of time, such as reading the clock or following the calendar. Teaching children to model their life based on time management and dates make them more committed towards their schedule, and being answerable to others. Help children to schedule their daily activities and categorize them in terms of play, study, relaxation, family time, reading time, bath and bedtime. Following the schedule will help them to understand how to follow rules and meet deadlines. Validate their success to help improve their self-esteem.

Organization Skills - Although children scatter their toys around the house, and expect mom and dad to keep them in place. This should be changed before they are ready to face the outside world. Teaching children that everything has its place, and keeping it where it belongs, is the key to good organizational skills.

Allocate laundry baskets, low level bookshelves, and separate boxes with pictures of their contents, so that children will know how to keep their stuff organized, and have a permanent place to study as well as play. Teaching them the value of each and every item that they possess makes them more responsible for their things.

Financial Management - Learning about the value of money comes naturally by teaching them to be responsible for their expenditures. One method for this is to give children their daily, weekly or monthly allowance, and when they shop they should be advised on how to compare between priority and luxury.

Children will never be able to handle money if they are not allowed to spend it. It is better that you allow your children to squander $20 of their own money and learn about impulsiveness, than to wait until they grow old and be shocked by their credit card debts. Teaching money management and saving would be great tools for any child to learn, and sadly many schools have little in the way of classes on this topic.

Mental Ability – Although the inheritance of intelligence is a debatable topic among many, it is possible for parents to increase the mental aptitude of their children by helping them learn effectively. You could introduce books and reading habits to your children. As you learn their best learning style –visual or audio, you can support the teacher's homework by working closely with your children and perhaps tailor their learning program accordingly.

With the awareness of various learning styles you could help your children learn in the way that helps them to grasp these new concepts and react accordingly. You can also help your children organize and schedule their own work schedule, so that they can see how order makes their life easier. Academic success, and learning information with new skills really boosts self-esteem in all ages of children and adults.

Insisting On Extra-curricular Activities

Sometimes children can be shy and introverted when it comes to mingling with other children. Gently insist that your children engage in extracurricular activities. When they meet other children of their age, they learn how to socialize among their age group and observe different things like –socialization, manners, popular games, clothing trends, new toys and school work. Since children cannot be forced to read the newspapers for general knowledge, yet this is the one way that you could help your child to be current in his or her age group.

Extracurricular activities also engage children in a lot of exercise which have been observed to accelerate brain power, grasping power, recognition of speech, and correction of attitudes. Engaging a child within the company of other children of his own age group will help your child be more comfortable and respect social values.

Keeping Your Child Motivated

Motivation and encouragement are the key factors behind a child's success. Do not punish your child or discourage him for every mistake he or she commits, but correct them and encourage them to do better the next time.

Encourage them, even in the most trivial matters, like washing the laundry, as it will make them feel more accountable. It will also give them a sense of hope that they can do it right the next time. A child or teen who feels confident and successful at home takes that confidence and healthy self-esteem with him/her into the "real world."

Self-Esteem Building Exercises made Especially for Teens

Positive Affirmations

Positive affirmations, sometimes simply referred to simply as affirmations, are when you "tell yourself" positive things with the expectation of making them become true at a future time. For the sake of this handbook, we're going to focus on positive affirmations to yourself. That being said, if you have this handbook as a way to help a friend or loved one, these affirmations can easily be reworded with "you," "yourself," etc. These can and do work over time.

Your subconscious mind can't tell fact from fiction, so repetition of positive affirmations is very effective in combating low self-esteem. While some of these will not be true at the time they're being recited, they will become true over time. Below are many examples of affirmations which can be used anytime of the day or evening. Find a safe place to say them out loud and say them to yourself ---in front of a mirror would be ideal. If one affirmation really resonates with you, then write it down on a card and keep it with you. Also, at the end of the book you will be directed to a place where you can download several Affirmations to help with your self-esteem.

- "I am relaxed"

- "I can breathe normally"

- "I am in control of my body"

- "I am in control of my mind"

- "I can accept reality and take it head on"

- "I am strong"

- "I love myself as I am"

- "I do not fear the future"

- "I am easily able to focus"

- "With every day that passes, I become more and more calm"

- "I can not be defeated by this, or anything else"

- "I look forward to each new day"

- "I am in control of my emotions"

- "I am in control of my actions"

- "I am confident"

- "I am absolutely normal"

- "I never give up"

- "I can do anything"

- "I accept myself as I am"

- "I am confident in my abilities"

- "I am not self-critical"

- "I am happy"

- "I am worthy of all that I seek"

- "I easily adjust to changes in my life"

- "All is right in my world"

- "People like me for who I am"

Meditation

Meditation is considered to be effective in dealing with self-esteem issues. It has been used for ages to discover inner peace and find mental discipline. It can help to fight anxiety, help with physical healing, allows the individual to focus on the here-and-now, and even become calmer. Various types of meditation techniques exist. The next section describes just a few of them.

Meditation techniques are available through websites, classes, CDs, DVDs, books and directly from professionals. You can even go to YOUTUBE and find a vast number of meditations to practice. The categories that could boost your knowledge and practice in meditation found onYouTube are: Guided Imagery, Guided Meditation, Creative Visualization, Guided Visualization, Hypnosis, Self-Hypnosis, Meditation, and many more.

- **Zen Meditation** – This type of meditation sometimes uses visualizations and, as shown in the photograph above, integrates your posture and your breathing. Its goal is to raise the level of your self-awareness and force the negative thoughts out and away from you.

Concentrate deliberately on your breathing. Slow it down and take deep breaths. This causes the brain to enter a tranquil state and calm you.

- **Meditation With a Mantra** – This form of meditation uses the repetition of a word or phrase many times in order to achieve a state of peace and the ability to view your negative thoughts "from afar" so that you can focus on observing them rather than living them.

- **Mindfulness Meditation** – Having its roots in Buddhism, this type of meditation focuses on you becoming *more* focused on your feelings and thoughts so that you *can* live in the here-and-now. Essentially, it's a form of facing your anxiety head on and trying to conquer it in a peaceful way.

Those who wish to try meditation as a form of dealing with their self-concept can learn through the many readily-available web sites, YouTube Videos, DVDs, books, articles and yoga studios that teach the different methods. Two examples from the internet follow. You may click on the link, or paste the link address into your browser.

http://www.bing.com/videos/search?q=Self+Esteem+Meditati ons&&view=detail&mid=D4C8AC12AF1B4EB8FB01D4C8 AC12AF1B4EB8FB01&rvsmid=EE578E7B4DCF7CC9FB49 EE578E7B4DCF7CC9FB49&fsscr=0&FORM=VDFSRV
Feel better about yourself – Increase Self Confidence – for Teens.

http://www.bing.com/videos/search?q=Self+Esteem+Meditati
ons&&view=detail&mid=2DE729C7CE4C0A1838FA2DE72
9C7CE4C0A1838FA&rvsmid=EE578E7B4DCF7CC9FB49E
E578E7B4DCF7CC9FB49&fsscr=-1485&FORM=VDFSRV

Improve your Self Image and Self-Esteem Meditation.

Exercise

Exercise releases endorphines, the feel good hormone. When we exercise it not only helps our body, but it helps our mood, our attitude and our self-esteem. Most of us are aware that if we look better, we feel better about ourselves.

What kind of excercise would be best to improve a child's self-esteem? Pick exercises that can be done with little chance of failure. If a parent exercises with their child, make sure to validate their good work and effort. Exercises done in groups of like-minded children would be great to do. Examples might be swimming classes, or martial arts. Cycling with family members or friends, and even jump-roping are also great activities to do.

The exercise or exercises chosen need not be competitive. If they are then there might be a need to check and see that they are not competing to seek inappropriate validation.

Here are some great stretching exercise links. Either click the link or paste the link into your browser:

http://www.bing.com/images/search?q=stretching+exercises&qpvt=stretching+exercises&FORM=IGRE

http://www.mayoclinic.com/health/stretching/SM00043

http://www.ehow.com/sports/fitness/stretching/

Getting Out of Our Heads

Guided Imageries or guided meditations get us out of our heads. We need to get out of our heads to really see and understand our behaviors. The problem is that many of us don't understand that some of our behaviors are unconscious. Bringing our behaviors into our conscious awareness takes time and effort, and usually guidance.

One of the most chronic issues of our time is low self-worth. (Self-worth is the same as self-esteem) This is an important issue which can cause tremendous limitations and problems as we age. We tend to replay in our heads, over and over again how unworthy we are, and why we are unworthy. These thoughts may have been told to us as children, or we just formulated these thoughts based on the way we were treated. We might also have had faulty perceptions of how people have thought of us, based on impaired social skills or perhaps low levels of depression or anxiety.

Practicing meditation or guided imagery is a healthy and safe way of escaping the sound of those negative voices. It is also free, and you can do it anywhere. The more you practice meditating or doing a guided imagery, the more peaceful you can become, as you will be detaching from the energy of those negative past voices and experiences. You can find many links at the end of this book to sites which offer free Guided Imagery And Meditations.

Most people "medicate" their low self-worth with a behavior which could easily become addictive. Find healthier alternatives!

https://www.youtube.com/watch?v=eCgPjj4ShAQ
Meditation to Quiet Busy Minds

Journaling

There are no hard and fast rules about how to journal, and there are thousands of "experts" out there suggesting that you do it this way or that. It is suggested that you Google journaling, and read the suggestions or techniques of different people. This author suggests that journaling is a process best done when it is done at the same time daily, for about 15 or 20 minutes. It can be done with pen to paper, the way the author prefers, or finger to computer keys and a word document. It also can be done with crayons or markers on blank paper for the younger children.

So why is journaling so highly suggested for children and teens to improve self-esteem? It offers them a view into their inner selves, a little bit at a time, in the privacy of their own home. It requires no therapist, yet may reveal information to share with a therapist or parents. Their thoughts and their feelings have a place to come out and be seen, instead of being trapped in their heads and their hearts. They will get to know themselves better, and probably see when they are whining and being a victim, and when they are empowered and making progress.

A journal is private. No one should see it. Any inspiration they get from it is a gift, and any "garbage" they dump is also a gift. These are private gifts. If they choose to share their journals with you, make it a "sacred" act. This means that this is a very special, special act on their part.

There are no rules to how to write, just write. There is a lot of activity that has gone on in their heads that has led your child to feel badly about himself/herself. So now is the time to get in touch with those negative voices or limited beliefs and see them written out, so that they can more easily dispute these thoughts. If a child is too young to journal, use a group of drawings, perhaps in a blank coloring book, or on blank paper kept together, as this can provide great relief and insight.

If you really can't think of anything to write then:

- Start writing a personal timeline of your life from as early as you can remember.
- Start a separate journal containing your gratitude for each day.
- Start writing out some grief letters to people who have passed away or moved away, saying what you never got to say to them.
- Have a pity party for yourself, and whine, whine, whine about why your life is so bad today.
- Write a letter (don't send it) in your journal to each of the people who have touched you and helped you on your journey from childhood to today.
- Write an anger letter (don't send it) to each person for whom you still have some resentment and bitterness stored deep inside you.
- Make a success list.
- Write how you would like to change your views of yourself and the world….

These are only some suggestions. If journaling ever triggers deep emotions in a child or teenager, then hopefully they can turn to their parents or someone else who they feel safe to talk with, and share what they are feeling.

Creative Visualization (Guided Imagery)

Many people believe there is great power in creative visualization. This is the process where someone used a CD, or DVD to guide them through an imaginative exercise. The purpose in this case would be to close your eyes and visualize yourself happy, competent, likeable, and participating with others.

There are many quality CDs and DVDs available to guide someone through a Creative Visualization. The key is to find a voice that you like and an imagery that fits your needs. Go to YouTube for the best selection of Guided Imageries, or Guided Meditations with many voices and techniques from which to choose.

https://www.youtube.com/watch?v=QFvelHlN9Rw A Guided Relaxation Session on Self-Esteem

https://www.youtube.com/watch?v=t7dEiclZP60 Guided Meditation to improve your Self Image and Self Esteem

Following is an example of a script for improving self-image. If you like it you could record it or have someone else record it for you to listen to in a quiet and safe place:

Improving Self-Image Script

"Find a comfortable place to relax, and make sure your arms and legs are uncrossed... become aware of your breath...and let's begin by taking three slow, deep breaths... Now close your eyes... and let the muscles in and around your eyes relax, and let your eyelids relax... and continue to let your eyelids relax...Let them relax so much that they won't work, even if you tried... Now let that relaxation flow up to your forehead and scalp.

Now let that relaxation flow out to your cheeks, and mouth, and chin... Let that relaxation flow down from your eyes, over your torso, and all the way down to your feet. Just allow the relaxation to take over your entire body now as you let go... just let go...

I'm going to count down from 10 to 1, and with each descending number, feel a wave of relaxation flowing over you, and flowing through you, relaxing every muscle, every tissue, every cell.

10... 9, feel the waves of relaxation...

8... 7, feel the relaxation flowing through you...

6... 5, more and more relaxed...

4... 3...letting go of today and relaxing more and more...

2... 1...very relaxed and comfortable...

Now scan your body and search for any remaining pockets of tension and on your next few exhales, exhale that tension that is stored in any muscles or tissues, exhale it right out... more and more relaxed with every gentle breath you take... more and more relaxed with every gentle breath you take... Now keeping your eyes closed, become aware of an image screen in front of your forehead, and on this image screen is your private showing of a wonderful healing image.

The first image I'd like you to visualize is that of a very secret or special place that only you can go to. It may be a forest or a pond, a beach or a field, a special room or a mountain. Whatever it is you have visualized, become aware of the colors in your special place, become aware of the three dimensions all around you, as you are now in your special place; relaxing, more and more with every breath...

This special place is a place for you to do some inner work, some healing...While relaxing in your special place I'm going to say statements to you, and as I say each statement, affirm it to be true by saying it to yourself, in your mind. Know these things to be true! There is no reason to think about these statements, so just let your conscious mind drift off. Just feel them, feel them opening up every cell of your being, cleansing and healing.

"Every day in every way, I am getting better and better..."

"Every day in every way, I am getting better and better..."

"Every day I am growing to know and accept myself more and more..."

"Every day I am growing to know and accept myself more and more..."

"Every day I am growing to love myself more and more..."

"Every day I am growing to love myself more and more..."

"Love is the opposite of fear. Where there's fear there is no love..."

"Love is the opposite of fear. Where there's fear there is no love..."

"My loving thoughts chase away all fear..."

"My loving thoughts chase away all fear..."

Know that every cell of your body has intelligence and can open up to relax to healing and cleansing... and every gentle breath takes you deeper and deeper relaxed. Every gentle breath takes you deeper and deeper relaxed.

Become aware now on your image screen in front of your head the image of a beautiful mansion-- a mansion of your design. It can be one that you've seen before, or just one you're creating right now... Slowly approach the mansion from the front, and enter the front door... and step into the foyer or the entrance of this wondrous mansion, and walk around and see the beautiful furniture, the paintings, the decorations...

Become aware of a beautiful staircase leading up to the second floor... Now proceed up this staircase and know in your heart that wonderful things await you at the top of these stairs.

*As you reach the top, you are aware of many doors with signs on them... The door that attracts you most is the **Relaxation Room**. So enter into it now and see the beautiful Jacuzzi with the water gently moving. Disrobe now and step into the Jacuzzi, and feel how different this water feels, so silky and soft. As it flows gently over your skin, you feel the relaxing effects on your skin, and you feel your cells being cleansed, and you know now this is not just ordinary water.*

This is magical, mystical water... And you feel the water flowing past the surface of the skin and down through the tissues, and

71

muscles and the bones... all of your cells....Now you feel your cells being opened and cleansed of toxins and residue which is unnecessary... Feel your organs being cleansed. Feel the water flowing through every part of your body. Just let go and release those toxins, those poisons, those tensions. Just exhale now and let go...(pause)

Now relaxed and refreshed, step out of the Jacuzzi and put your clothes back on and exit the relaxation room to the hallway. In the hallway see another room with a sign saying **Media Room.** *Enter into this room now and see all of the equipment. All of the equipment that you could possibly want in a mixed media room - computers, books, stereos, CD equipment, paint, easels, drawing pads, pencils, clay – everything that any artist would need to create.*

Look around now and add any other equipment that you would like to have... Now sit down in front of a clump of clay, or in front of an easel, or a computer, and create a 3-dimensional ***image of you*** *as you would like to be. Perhaps you would like to be slimmer, or stronger, or more confident.*

Create that image now... Make sure you put in every detail... including the expressions on your face... See this completed 3-dimensional you as not only a possibility of what you can become, but this is who you really are underneath the layer of limiting thoughts and emotions which you have stored. (pause)

See yourself in this figure as the real you. Now take that 3-dimensional figure and add more color to the scene...turn up the light and make the image brighter... and make the whole image larger... and as you observe this ***"REAL YOU"*** *– brighter, more colorful – add the emotion of* ***desire***....

As you see this image, desire this image to be you. Feel that desire in your chest now. Look at the image and feel that desire. You wish to be this image. Feel it... now add a second emotion, the emotion of **belief.** Believe this **IS** really you, right now. Believe it. Feel that in your chest. Feel the belief that this is you... and now a third emotion, add **expectance.** Expect this image to be the real you, right now. Expect it, just as if you were expecting a wonderful gift. For now you realize that this is a gift, and you hold it within you...

Now remember this image and the three emotions of desire, belief and expectancy. And know that <u>the subconscious does</u> <u>everything in its power to create what it perceives you to be,</u> <u>and right now it perceives you to be</u> this image... The more you see this image, the more powerful this image has an effect on your subconscious.

The more desire, belief, and expectancy you have, the more power the change will be... Now as you look at this image, say the following statements to yourself: *"I believe in myself." "I believe in myself." "I am capable." "I am capable." "I am lovable.""I am lovable." "I am confident." "I am confident." "I feel good about myself." "I feel good about myself."*

You may come back to this special mansion any time. You may go on to the media room and create other images. This image you see now is the real you, and is manifesting right now. Come back to this room often, and every time you do this exercise, you will go deeper and deeper relaxed....

Slowly now, we're going to come back to this room where you are. As I count from 1 to 5, you'll have a choice of opening your *eyes at the number 5, or going on to a deeper state of relaxation and sleep.*

1, Feeling better than you have felt in a long time...

2, Believing in how lovable and confident your really are...

3, Start becoming aware of your surroundings...

4, Feel a coolness flowing over your eyes, like they're being bathed by a mountain stream...

5, Eyes open when you're ready, feeling refreshed and relaxed, like you've just had a wonderful massage and shower."

Community Groups or Extra-Curricular Activities at School and at Church

Many communities have cub scout, girl scout, and boy scout groups available. These groups have been around for years and have great adult supervision. There are also after school programs for every age group that offer anything from art to sports.

While adult supervision doesn't always guarantee no teasing or name-calling, it is usually a much better place for your child to be than an unsupervised park or playground. Successes in activities with others, especially if they are validated, really help develop a healthy self-esteem.

Conclusion

As you have read through this book, you have learned how self-esteem is formed. You now know the effects on the life of someone who has developed a good self-esteem versus someone who has developed an unhealthy self-esteem. You also know how vulnerable self-esteem is to a child and adolescent. You know that you, as the parent, have a key role in development of your child's self-esteem.

The challenge to you now is to stay conscious of your role in helping others develop a positive self-esteem, and not only your children. Positive Self-Esteem is linked to a much more productive and happy life for most people.

Take the time to smile and validate others' good behavior, whether it is your child or a clerk at the store. Give compliments freely. Express gratitude as a natural way of interacting with others. <u>Stop your verbal and non-verbal criticisms and judgments of others, and try to only see the good.</u> Even your body language sends a message of acceptance or judgment.

We don't develop our self-esteem in a vacuum. Everyone around us has some influence in it. Please be a positive influence where ever you can. Continue your learning by exploring the Links, Videos and Apps listed at the end of this book.

Self-Esteem Enhancers.......

These Self-Esteem Enhancers are actually "affirmations" which are deeply rooted in history....

The theory is that we have become programmed by parents, siblings, society, television, the internet, the media, etc., and this programming has led to our attitudes about ourselves and others. This programming is very often negative, leaving us with a negative self-image.

By taking a positive statement, such as a Self-Esteem Enhancer attached, and repeating it for 7 to 21 days, we begin to change that programming. <u>The more we repeat the statement, and the more feeling behind it, the stronger and quicker the results.</u>

Thinking the statement you pick for 10 times each day is <u>okay,</u> saying it out loud 10 times is <u>good,</u> and saying out loud it and writing it 10 times daily <u>is excellent</u>. One way to begin reprogramming yourself is to mentally repeat the Self-Esteem Enhancer as many times as you can during the day when you have a few free minutes.

****

<u>Directions</u>: Say the Self-Esteem Enhancer which you choose, 10 times in the morning just after rising, and 10 times in the evening just before bed for 7 to 21 days. Say it out loud if at all possible. Looking in a mirror while saying it, gives extra power to the activity. Also, the more times you say it, the quicker and more powerful the results. Concentrate on one Self-Esteem Enhancer at a time for best results. Also, don't share your Self-Esteem

Enhancer with anyone else, as you don't want any chance of someone's negative thoughts or comments weakening your efforts to make a positive change in yourself. Good Luck and Bon Voyage on your journey to loving yourself more completely..........

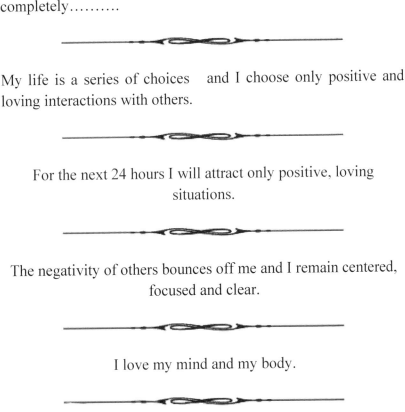

My life is a series of choices and I choose only positive and loving interactions with others.

For the next 24 hours I will attract only positive, loving situations.

The negativity of others bounces off me and I remain centered, focused and clear.

I love my mind and my body.

I leave my negative self-image behind me and see only a positive love-filled me.

Others are attracted to my loving, peaceful nature. I radiate contentment.

My loving thoughts chase away all fear.

I easily release all anger in an appropriate way.

I release and let go of any need to feel guilty.

I radiate peace and contentment.

I forgive myself for living in shame and guilt and easily release the need to feel these limiting feelings.

I release those who I feel have limited or victimized me, by understanding, loving and forgiving them.

I choose peace, love and joy as my companions today.

The child within me plays in the moment and experiences freedom and joy.

This is my day to feel peace, love and harmony in all that I say and do.

I deserve to experience peace, love and harmony.

I am worthy of love.

I am honest, open and loving in all that I say and do.

I believe in ME!

I like myself.

I am loveable.

I feel good about myself.

I have faith in myself.

80

I love myself.

I am confident.

I now accept myself and others exactly as we are.

Every day I grow to love myself more and more.

I believe in myself.

My thoughts are positive and loving, and I am always attracting this in others.

I am beautiful and loveable and have a great deal to share with others.

Every day, in every way, I grow more and more positive, calmer and at peace with myself.

I am a positive influence in all situations I encounter.

I am lovable and capable.

The child within me finds healthy ways of play and self-expression.

I believe in ME!

I allow myself to relax and be at peace.

I am a positive influence in all situations I encounter.

I am positive and loving.

I am source of great joy and creativity.

Every day I grow to know and accept myself more and more.

I am beautiful and lovable and have a great deal to share with others.

Every day, in every way, I am getting better and better.

References

Baccus, J. R., Baldwin, M. W., Packer, D. J. (2004): *Increasing Implicit Self-Esteem through Classical Conditioning,* Psychological Science, Vol. 15, No. 7.

Baumeister, R. F. (2005): *Rethinking Self-Esteem, Why Nonprofits Should Stop Pushing Self-Esteem and Start Endorsing Self-Control,* Stanford Social Innovation Review, Winter 2005

Baumeister, R. F., Campbell, J. D., Krueger, J. I., Vohs, K. D. (2003): *Does High Self-Esteem Cause Better Performance, Interpersonal Success, Happiness, or Healthier Lifestyles?* Psychological Science in the Public Interest, Vol. 4, No. 1, May 2003

Brandon, Nathaniel, (1994): *The Six Pillars of Self-Esteem*

Brown, J. D., Marshall, M. A. (2006): *The Three Faces of Self-Esteem,* IN: Kernis, M. (Ed.): Self-esteem: Issues and Answers, New York, Psychology Press, pp. 4-9

Erol, R. Y., Orth, U. (2011): *Self-Esteem Development from Age 14 to 30: A Longitudinal Study,* Journal of Personality and Social Psychology, Vol. 101, No. 3, 607-619

Mills, D. (2003): *Overcoming "Self-Esteem", Why Our Compulsive Drive for "Self-Esteem" is Anxiety-Provoking, Socially inhibiting, and Self-Sabotaging,* Albert Ellis Institute, 2003

Links

Article: 11 Facts about Teens and Self-Esteem
http://www.dosomething.org/tipsandtools/11-facts-about-teens-and-self-esteem

Article: How Can I Improve My Self-Esteem?
http://kidshealth.org/teen/your_mind/emotions/self_esteem.html

Article: A Positive Image and Self-Esteem
http://www.pamf.org/teen/life/depression/selfesteem.html

Article: Adolescence and Self-Esteem
http://www.psychologytoday.com/blog/surviving-your-childs-adolescence/201009/adolescence-and-self-esteem

Article: How to Raise Girls with Healthy Self-Esteem
http://www.aboutourkids.org/articles/how_raise_girls_healthy_selfesteem

Article: Self-Esteem and Anxiety in Kids
http://www.empoweringparents.com/Self-Esteem-And-Anxiety-In-Teens.php

Article: 10 Signs of Low Self-Esteem in Teenagers
http://understandingteenagers.com.au/blog/2010/08/10-signs-of-low-self-esteem-in-teenagers/

Article: Self-Esteem and Confidence
http://www.cyh.com/HealthTopics/HealthTopicDetails.aspx?p=243&np=293&id=2161

Article: Pre-Teen Self-Esteem is a Direct Reflection of How a Child Feels About Himself http://www.preteen-thru-teenage-parenting-action-guide.com/preteen-self-esteem.html

85

Article: Body Image and Self-Esteem
http://kidshealth.org/teen/your_mind/body_image/body_image.html

Article: Low Self-Esteem in Teenagers
http://www.professorshouse.com/Family/Teens/Articles/Low-Self-Esteem-in-Teenagers/

Article: Guided Imagery
http://www.Livestrong.com/article/164001-visualization-guided-imagery/

Guided Imagery Explained "Guided Imagery
**Meditation Oasis Website for Information and Select
Meditations:** http://www.meditationoasis.com
YouTube Guided Imagery Selection:
https://www.google.com/webhp?sourceid=chrome-instant&ion=1&espv=2&ie=UTF-8#q=guided%20imagery%20%20site%3Ayoutube.com

Article: 6 Tips to Improve Self-Esteem
http://psychcentral.com/blog/archives/2011/10/30/6-tips-to-improve-your-self-esteem/

Article: How to Improve your self-esteem: 12 Powerful Tips
http://www.positivityblog.com/index.php/2013/09/11/improve-self-esteem/

Video: 10 Tips for Improved Self Esteem
https://www.youtube.com/watch?v=Oc-B536E6MY

Article: Teens...How can I improve my Self-Esteem?
http://teenshealth.org/en/teens/self-esteem.html

Article: 13 Tips to Building Self Esteem
http://thinksimplenow.com/happiness/the-art-of-building-self-esteem/

YouTube Videos

https://www.youtube.com/watch?v=zq-fSpFhNYw "3 Ways to boost your Self Esteem"

https://www.youtube.com/watch?v=Oc-B536E6MY "10 Tips for Improving Self Esteem"

https://www.youtube.com/watch?v=FeLpvgAVtU8 "Self Esteem Understanding & Fixing Low Self-Esteem"

https://www.youtube.com/watch?v=AvIKj6R3axE "How to Stop Caring What People Think"

https://www.youtube.com/watch?v=dhuabY4DmEo "HOW TO BUILD SELF ESTEEM - THE SIX PILLARS OF SELF-ESTEEM BY NATHANIEL BRANDEN ANIMATED BOOK REVIEW"

YouTube Guided Imagery Selection:
https://www.google.com/webhp?sourceid=chrome-instant&ion=1&espv=2&ie=UTF-8#q=guided%20imagery%20%20site%3Ayoutube.com

https://www.youtube.com/watch?v=Ybkh4ekVWug "How does EMDR work?"

https://www.youtube.com/watch?v=AwRLrnlSl78&list=PL526PJmJkdkS5wVkYSLwKx0vjLtYD5m8Y "EMDR – Smile and feel Positive."

https://www.youtube.com/watch?v=v5IRwMqZSMg "EMDR – Be Positive 2"

Apps for easy use

http://kidsrelaxation.com/uncategorized/7-apps-to-help-kids-relax/ "7 apps to Help Kids Relax"

http://www.adaa.org/finding-help/mobile-apps "Mental Health Apps"

https://www.anxiety.org/4-apps-for-anxiety-and-depression "Reduce anxiety and depression by using these apps."

http://psychcentral.com/blog/archives/2013/09/20/top-10-free-mental-health-apps/ "Top 10 free mental health apps."

https://play.google.com/store/apps/details?id=com.zalebox.self.esteem.building.guide Self-Esteem Building Apps

https://itunes.apple.com/us/app/self-esteem-daily-affirmations/id467210522?mt=8 Self Esteem Daily Affirmations

https://itunes.apple.com/us/app/build-self-esteem-hypnosis/id741949224?mt=8

Building Self-Esteem Hypnosis –Guided Meditation with Healing Affirmations to Build Self-Confidence and Motivation

http://www.shaanhaider.com/2012/06/best-self-esteem-improving-iphone-apps.html Top 3 Self-Esteem Improving iPhone and iPad Apps

http://www.huffingtonpost.com/fueled/strut-your-stuff-5-apps-t_b_5647016.html **5 Apps that can Help Build Self-Esteem**

http://mindfitapp.com/2014/09/26/improving-self-esteem/ **Improving your Self-Esteem app**

Books and E-Books from RLT Publishing

"Overcoming Anger in Teens and Pre-Teens: A Parent's Guide"

"Tragedy, Trauma and Loss in Teens and Pre-Teens: Healing the Wounds"

"Overcoming Drug and Alcohol Problems in Teens and Pre-Teens: A Parent's Guide"

"Overcoming ADHD in Teens and Pre-Teens: A Parent's Guide"

"Overcoming Anxiety in Teens and Pre-Teens: A Parent's Guide"

"Overcoming Depression in Teens and Pre-Teens: A Parent's Guide"

"Overcoming Obesity in Teens and Pre-Teens: A Parent's Guide"

"Overcoming Self-Esteem Problems in Teens and Pre-Teens: A Parent's Guide"

"Tech Etiquette: OMG"

"Guided Imagery"

"Gay Men's Guide to Love and Relationships"

"Sexual Identity? Moving from Confusion to Clarity"

"The Traveling Parent"

Addiction in the LGBTQ Community"

"Validation Addiction: Please Make Me Feel Worthy"

"Addicted Physicians: Healing the Healer"

"Addicted Nurses: Healing the Caregiver"

"Addicted Pilots: Flight Plan for Recovery"

"Addicted Pharmacists: Healing the 'Medicine Man'"

Tragedy, Trauma and Loss: Healing the Emotional Wounds"

If you have enjoyed this book, please go back and <u>do a</u> <u>REVIEW</u> on it. Reviews increase the exposure of books. We would like more people to read this to help them on their journey of improving their child's self-esteem.

Thank you........RLT Publishing

About the Author

Dr. Richard Travis is a Psychotherapist who is in Private Practice in Fort Lauderdale, Florida. In his psychotherapy practice, he has worked with general issues in the population, such as depression, anxiety, and relationship problems. He has also worked with a great many gay men and the HIV population for over twenty (25) years. His specialty in Addictions has allowed him to see how addictions have complicated and destroyed relationships, ruined people's health, and made chaos of their financial situations.

He received his first Master's Degree at Edinboro University of Pennsylvania in Education. He received his second Master's Degree in Counselor Education at Florida Atlantic University in Boca Raton, Florida. He received his Doctorate in Higher Education/Counseling Psychology at Florida International University in Miami, Florida. He has Specialties in Addictions, including State, National and International certifications. He has worked with several people in the healthcare industry who have been in Addiction Monitoring Programs, and currently facilitates several groups a month with professionals being monitored by state and federal agencies.

Dr. Travis has taught classes with every age level of student in Pennsylvania, Michigan and Florida, including teaching graduate Social Work classes at Florida International University in Miami. He has also published several articles on the website Ezinearticles.com.

An Excerpt from "Overcoming Drug and Alcohol Problems in Teens and Pre-Teens: A Parent's Guide" by Dr. Richard L. Travis

"Why Some Children Start Using Drugs

There is a strange, and yet very commonplace opinion that only children from poor and needy families are at risk to become drug or alcohol addicted. Unfortunately, this is not true, and alcohol or drug abuse depends on different factors, and social status is not the most important one. One of the main reasons why children start abusing drugs is **the environment**. If your kid's friends have alcohol or drug problems and they hang out with bad or troubled teens – there is a great possibility that your child will start doing the same. Living in a rough neighborhood could also lead to problems with drugs and alcohol as well.

Previous family history of substance usage.

If someone in your family is or was abusing drugs and a child witnessed that process – he will consider it to be normal and will likely start taking drugs as well. Also, countless studies have proven the genetic link in terms of addiction. Teenagers with parents, grandparents or other relatives who had a drinking or drug problem are more likely to develop alcoholism themselves.

Conflict at home.

If parents live separately, fight regularly, have recently divorced or do not pay much attention to keeping the family harmonious and together, then their children are influenced by an unhealthy family environment. These children might start abusing drugs and alcohol to self-medicate their pain, while others will do it as an act of rebellion against the parents who are causing them stress."

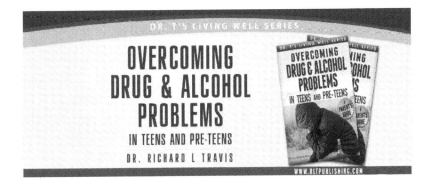

Made in the USA
San Bernardino, CA
05 February 2017